Finding Yourself:

Your 7 Step Guide to Living Your Best Life

Janet Martin

TABLE OF CONTENTS

Free Book Download

Improve the quality of your life and harness the power you have within you.

*****

Start your journey of self discovery and improvement with the modern, research-backed and life-changing book "How To Journal For Mental Health". Grab your FREE copy now: www.success-all.com/findingyourself

Disclaimer

INTRODUCTION

Each day, we're made to believe that we are being provided with the best tools to make life easier. The latest mobile phones are advertised to make communication better. Productivity apps are there to make work more efficient. Shopping trends have convinced us that our work-from-home setups are part of our new normal.

Everything is convenient, automated, delegated. You're not supposed to be worrying about any of that anymore, they say... You've found the secret to a happy, productive, and successful you, they say.

And yet, you find yourself feeling overwhelmed every morning and fatigued every night (or even the other way round!). Anxious thoughts replay in your mind, and the energy you exert doesn't seem to reap any rewards.

The global pandemic has definitely changed us all. Some of us had to undergo major life adjustments. Pivoting our careers. Giving up our homes. Switching family roles and setups.

For some it has been for the better; for others, for the worse. Many of us have spent a great deal of time just trying to find some sense of stability during this tumultuous period.

And just when you think you've put everything in order, for some reason, you get the feeling that it's not enough. That you're not supposed to be in this position. That things are not moving.

But let me tell you something. **You are exactly where you need to be right now.**

Whatever you've worked for, whatever relationships you've formed, whatever opportunities have come and gone; they have brought you here.

Whatever goals you are aiming for, whatever dreams you have, and whatever happiness you envision; they will all happen because you are where you are today.

The positive of being faced with a crossroads in our life, or even reaching a dead end, is that it forces us to take our life into our own hands and act.

You're exactly where you need to be, and the perfect time to start living on your own terms is **now**.

I'm so happy you've picked up this book as a step towards taking action. Here, I will guide you through overcoming common external and internal blocks, learning to be kinder to yourself, and taking the next steps towards living life exactly your way. By the end of this book, you'll be able to help yourself become a more authentic you.

I hope this helps you in your journey towards a better, more fulfilled, more empowered life. Onward!

ABOUT THE AUTHOR

Before becoming an author and founding Success All, a startup that offers products and services to bring out your empowered self, Janet Martin lived a dynamic and exciting life working in the music industry. From putting on shows at Radio City Music Hall in NYC to attending the Cannes Film Festival and GRAMMY awards, she eventually took a pause to focus on her growing family.

Over the past decade, Janet has written extensively for parenting blogs and started two companies, including web design and graphic design contracts for charitable organizations.

Janet's personal mission is to empower as many people as she can to become the best version of themselves. She's particularly passionate about the areas of empowerment, mindset, emotions, motivation, business, finances, relationships, and spirituality.

With the jet-setting life behind her, she has found her perfect home on the banks of the River Thames in South London. She enjoys supporting people with difficult pasts, the marginalized and under-represented.

In her spare time she's boxing at her local gym, taking calm walks in nature, reflecting during quiet moments of meditation and, finally, sharing an irreplaceable bond with her multi-marathon-running husband and her two incredible young daughters.

You'll find more of her personal and heartwarming stories within the pages of this book.

To learn more about Success All, visit our website or follow on instagram @successall1

STEP 1

ENJOY THE JOURNEY

Life has never been a straight path—we've all had our ups and downs, road bumps and dead ends, thrills and accidents. As we get older and add more experiences into our bags, it can become increasingly difficult to take risks, make ambiguous decisions, and embrace the unknown. After all, the future should be certain, right?

Say you're holding the steering wheel of your life. If you were to take control of your life today, where would you go? How would you do it?

Would you take a short and safe drive around the block? Do you have a far-off destination in mind—the furthest your tank will take you? Are you going to roam with no fixed stop in mind until you find a spot you like? Will you go quickly or slowly?

I don't have the answer for you. No one does! In fact, today's answer may be very different from tomorrow's.

The future is never certain. You can make all the plans you want, but nobody knows what tomorrow will bring. It's the journey, not the destination, that carries the real adventure of life.

So, what's important is to **enjoy the journey**.

In truth, the moment you leave your comfort zone, you're already a better person.

Back in 2003, I left London to study for an MBA in Atlanta, Georgia. Despite London being the best city in the world (I'm a little biased), I knew in my gut that some exciting opportunities existed in my new home in the US of A.

I arrived with just two suitcases, a copy of "The Magic of Thinking Big" by David J. Schwartz, and a rough idea of where I would sleep for the first night. My plane landed on a balmy summer day and I was picked up from the airport by one of my new classmates—just the beginning of the amazing "southern hospitality" I experienced throughout my time in Atlanta.

All I could hope was that I'd not made the wrong decision, and to be honest, I was absolutely petrified that it wouldn't work out and I'd return to London a failure. How wrong I was! I think this was one of the best experiences of my life for teaching me that the fear that accompanies coming out of my comfort zone is the best kind of fear I could possibly feel.

"Enjoying the journey" can be easier said than done for many of us. It's perfectly natural to feel afraid, anxious, and even hesitant about moving forward. To "enjoy the journey" feels vague and almost hedonistic, so let me share with you some concrete ways you can apply this to whatever situation you're in.

Take on a positive attitude. In whatever endeavor you begin, apply the mindset that, although it will not be smooth sailing, **you will have fun**, nonetheless.

We tend to take ourselves a little too seriously. You might be extracting down to the very last detail every single task that needs to be accomplished to make the event you're planning perfect. Or perhaps you are racing for that promotion at work, to the point where you overload yourself with tasks and are on your best, pristine behavior, to the point of robotic stiffness, forgetting to smile and relax.

Setting absurdly high standards for ourselves and creating too many tasks will only cause us to hyperfocus on the impossible. When we aspire to perfection, any little roadblock that comes our way becomes more difficult to overcome.

Keep your sense of humor, and approach new experiences with a childlike sense of wonder. Allow your creativity to flourish and accept the mistakes that will inevitably come. Embrace unfamiliarity and give yourself the grace to find your footing.

Each experience, whether positive or negative, will only make the story of your life richer and give you the wisdom, maturity, and skills to become a better person.

My actual qualification is an MBA in Marketing that was obtained in 2005, but essentially it's just a sheet of paper which I've (unfortunately) misplaced. However, that paper is nothing compared to the experiences that got me to my final qualification.

The late nights studying, the hustling to exist on low-paying campus jobs, my first encounters with gun culture... All those experiences were what made it fun. Not the actual final qualification.

Enjoying the journey also means **being mindful of the present moment**.

Surely, there are mistakes to look back on, regrets you carry with you, anxieties about the future, and anticipation for upcoming rewards. All of this is normal, but remember that we cannot change the past, and we cannot predict the future. We can just embrace the present moment.

Being aware of where you are at the moment means being mindful of what's around you. What does your path look like from where you stand? Did something unique happen to you today? How are you different from yesterday? And what can you do today to make tomorrow even better?

Look at where you are right now and take note of your growth and progress. You may feel like you're on the first page of a new chapter in your life. But, in the larger scheme of things, you are, perhaps, on the two-hundredth page and the twenty-third chapter in the story of your life. See how far you've come!

As you allow yourself to take on your experiences positively while living in the present moment, **gratitude will naturally come**.

Be thankful, not only for the triumphs, but for the challenges as well. Each moment is, after all, an opportunity.

None of this will be easy. Whatever path you choose, there will be uncertainties, roadblocks, and a multitude of problems to troubleshoot. Perhaps you will even have people around you who will not be supportive of your decisions. (When I first told my dad that I wanted to study in Atlanta, he said it was a terrible idea!)

None of this will be easy. But it will be yours to own.

None of this will be easy. But you can handle it with grace.

In the next chapter, let's talk about what happens when life gets too much to handle.

Take Action:

Stop whatever you're doing, plug in your headphones, and play your favorite song. Live in the song for the three-something minutes or so. Don't let your thoughts stray; just be in the moment. How did it feel? This is a simple exercise to get you started on practicing mindfulness. Every day, pause for a few moments to take a few mindful breaths, and focus all your thoughts on your body. Let your senses tell you where you are, what you see, how you're feeling.

Journal* Prompt:

Reflect on a special time in your life and one particular memory you are extremely grateful to have experienced. Write about it in detail.

(*If you prefer, substitute with a piece of paper/note taking app/email draft/voice note)

STEP 2

CALM YOURSELF

S tress. Just like you, I know what it feels like. Facing an unexpected traffic jam minutes before an important appointment. Staring at a full calendar and insisting I can strike off every task and attend every meeting despite it being logically impossible. Skipping valuable time with family and friends—and, most of all, myself—because work has consumed my energy meant for leisure and relaxation.

It happens to all of us. And most of the time, we don't even realize it's happening. I know I've been guilty of it. My body reacted as thoughts ran wild, and my heart began to race. The only way for me to unload all of this was to take my temper out on the first person I saw. I drowned myself in my thoughts, allowing the feeling of being overwhelmed to consume me, and refused to admit that I didn't have things under control.

I was excellent at denying I was stressed. After all, stress felt like such a dirty word to me. Admitting I was stressed meant admitting I was weak. I simply refused to believe I had too much on my plate.

The fact is, stress is a natural reaction of our body. When we're faced with a situation that feels new, threatening, or seemingly out of our control, stress can begin to manifest. Put simply, stress is just our body reacting to pressure.

When your brain detects a form of threat or pressure, it informs your adrenal glands. These glands then release adrenaline and cortisol, also known as stress hormones. It's these hormones that spread throughout your body and cause it to react during this period of "emergency".

These hormones are useful for priming your body to deal with a primal stressful situation, such as being chased, or having to think quickly to resolve a dangerous situation but are less helpful in an everyday environment when your body has nothing to expend them on.

There were many clear signs of my stress building up which only now, in hindsight, have I recognized and acknowledged. Stiff shoulders, clenched jaw, tight throat and hair loss are some of my "favorites"!

How does stress manifest for you?

When your brain sends a message to your heart, it begins pumping faster, and this can cause palpitations, which might lead to heavy breathing. Besides your body tensing up or shaking, you might also experience headaches, nausea, indigestion, and other digestive problems. Your emotions might overwhelm you, too: sudden outbursts and tantrums, crying, panic attacks.

Here's the thing: once stress takes over, it can become increasingly difficult to manage. You may not realize the indirect, but adverse, effects of these manifestations.

You might lose sleep, neglect some good habits, or even begin to crave or depend on vices. Relationships might start to get strained, and mental health begins to worsen.

But you can manage stress before it happens, or the moment you begin to observe the initial symptoms.

When my kids were very young, I remember feeling stressed out of my mind—but still in my denial phase. I had a newborn and a two-year-old toddler. To say it was overwhelming is an understatement! I honestly think I might still be recovering from mild "young family PTSD". My husband worked shifts during this period. Every six weeks, he would be working flat out for eight days in a row—rarely home and in no way able to help me out with the little ones.

During that time, I was pretty much solo with the kids. "Coincidentally", every six weeks, I would get a sore throat followed by a cold. Without fail. My body was sending me a very strong message that I was overwhelmed. My self-care routine was non-existent. Yet it took me a while to connect his shift pattern and my persistent colds.

When it finally hit me that this was how stress had begun manifesting, I learned to be better at observing the changes in my body, both internally and externally.

Try **checking in with yourself** every day, too. All the more if you're undergoing a particularly critical period in your life. Career shifts and working long hours, changing family setups and losing loved ones, experiencing illness and financial problems are just some of the possible issues. What emotions are you feeling? Is your skin breaking out? Are you getting enough sleep? How is your diet? If you begin to see patterns emerging, ask yourself what variables might have led to these physiological or behavioral changes.

Feed yourself some positive thoughts, celebrate triumphs, and process your thoughts and emotions to avoid feeling the burdens you might otherwise be facing. **Positive self-talk is a form of self-care.** So is allowing yourself at least a few minutes every day to relax. Calm your brain with deep breaths and perform activities that give you joy. Unplug from social media and give time to yourself to nourish your senses.

Develop good habits. By establishing a healthy routine for yourself, you avoid the risk of getting sucked into situations that might lead to increased stress. Don't worry if you miss today's exercise or sleep an hour later than scheduled—allow yourself some contingency. There's always tomorrow to start again!

When you're kind to yourself, when you listen to your body, and when you take control of your personal needs, you are taking the right strides towards **caring for yourself** and the people around you.

Today, I know that to give my family the best of me, I have to prioritize my health. Just as much as I pour love, care, and affection onto them, I need to do the same, if not more, for myself. When I detect signs of stress, I listen. Immediately. It's my body giving me a sign to up my self-care.

By taking care of my physical, mental, and emotional wellbeing, I'm making an effort towards having a happier and more authentic life. I'm making an effort towards **loving myself**.

Take care of yourself. It's a big world out there, and you need to be in the best shape to face it. Let's extract that a little more in the next step.

Take Action:

What makes up your daily routines? What tasks and actions do you habitually perform in the same order? Where can you incorporate a few minutes of extra "me time" into an existing routine? A body scrub in the shower? Re-routing your regular journey so that you can enjoy some time in a park? See how many you can think of and make them happen!

Journal Prompt:

Look back on the week that just passed. Were there moments that stressed you out? Can you see any patterns of behavior that are not serving you well? If you had a busy week, are there are some things you could spend less time on, which are unimportant or can be done in a more efficient way, which will then give you some spare time for something joyful? Finally, tell yourself you did a good job this week. Because truly, you did.

STEP 3

BE STRONGER THAN YOUR OBSTACLES

We can spend so much time and effort creating plans for our lives, envisioning the results of our goals being achieved. Of course, it's good to have a plan and create a roadmap for our careers and personal achievements. It creates a path that allows us to focus our priorities in the present to earn the results in the future.

But roadblocks are inevitable. And we're not always prepared for those challenges. We envision our wins without realizing that we will likely face some challenges. We'll fall, we'll make mistakes, we'll be faced with situations that we can't handle.

Something I've learned over time is that, when I'm met with such a hurdle, it doesn't mean I've reached a dead end.

Imagine stepping up to the door of a house you wish to enter. It's locked. What do you do? Do you turn back and return later? Do you give up entirely? Do you wait for someone with a key to open the door for you? Do you attempt all sorts of hacks to force the door open? Do you find another way in?

Your answer may vary because your next action depends on your level of comfort, given the situation you've been dealt with.

Whether you force the door depends on how urgent it is that you get inside – maybe there is someone injured in there. Whether you wait for someone with a key to come and open it will depend on whether you know the key is on its way, and how long you can afford to wait. Perhaps you don't really need to get into the house at all.

There will always be surprises and roadblocks along the way, but none of it should deter us from moving forward or pivoting when needed.

Don't give up—and if you do, know that there's always another path to take.

Most of us can relate to this more than we can imagine, especially in the last couple of years. Many of us had our own set of plans, routines, and goals back in January of 2020. We were looking forward to new beginnings, continuing our achievements, and leaving behind the unnecessary.

At the end of February 2020 (we all know what was on the way), I had been in discussions for months with a lovely little factory in China about them manufacturing a product I had worked very hard on. We had just finalized it, and I had sent over my 50% deposit.

Fast forward to one month later, and everything came to a halt. The pandemic hit. Bam! Months of hard work, planning, negotiating and, quite frankly, blood, sweat, and tears, all vanished in a matter of days as the world shut down.

I was devastated. Not only had I worked so hard to bring everything together, but I had also honestly put my best foot forward. I had a laser focus on my goal, had carefully researched and evaluated my business decisions. I even gave up my Netflix subscription to make sure there was only learning related to my new passion on my TV screen!

It feels like whiplash, doesn't it—when your hopes and expectations come crashing down. But as they say: when one door closes, another one opens. That image of you standing in front of a door that's been locked offers a number of opportunities to recalibrate, brainstorm, and even restart.

I decided not to stop, despite the obstacles I was facing. I knew that even though my new (old!) business idea had gone up in smoke, there were still plenty of opportunities to make a solid recovery. I enlisted a new business mentor to help me refocus and within a few months I had not only recovered, but improved on my previous model. I'd adapted to the new way of life both professionally and personally, and by 2022 had released four new products (the fifth of which you're reading now!).

Most of the time, it's not an external situation that prevents us from pursuing our goals. It's actually the expectations we put on ourselves. It's the desire for perfection, the illusion of success, the blinders we put on to have our eyes solely on that specific prize.

Having such a mindset only leads to exhaustion before we've taken even a few steps ahead. Going for 100% all the time puts a toll on our minds and bodies. Even dancers and stage performers will tell us that they don't give their 100% every night they perform. Instead, they have trained themselves to provide a worthy performance that presents the illusion of giving it their all.

Let me share with you some ways that might help you be prepared for the unexpected curveballs life might throw your way.

Know the difference between **working hard** and **working smart**. Working hard is putting all your efforts into your goal—which isn't bad to begin with, but can become unhealthy when you experience fatigue from overwhelming challenges. Working smart, on the other hand, is about pacing yourself and being able to look at your tasks from a broader perspective. Working smart will allow you to take breaks and step back to monitor your goals and your wellbeing, as well as the situation around you.

Ask for help. Delegate. Remember: you can't do it all! And that's okay.

Recognize that **some things are beyond your control**. Instead, **focus on what you can change**. Most likely, these are not external situations per se, but rather, how you react to them. Be mindful of your knee-jerk reactions. Ignore any hate or judgment that comes at you. Be grateful for the positive things going on in your life.

When we're faced with a locked door, the first step, ironically, is to **take a step back**. Think, look at the larger perspective, and then figure out your next plan of action.

Life is indeed full of twists and turns. There's never a straight path to success.

It would be good to ask yourself, too, how you would define success. You'll find that it's never really about winning the grand prize, but rather about the contentment of knowing you've done what you can to get wherever you're at. It's about picking yourself up from the challenges you've faced and mistakes that have been made. It's about making the best darn lemonade with whatever lemons life has given you.

Because when we're doing meaningful work, no amount of rain should stop us, right? Let's move on to the next step.

"Success is a peace of mind which is a direct result of self-satisfaction in knowing you did your best to become the best you are capable of becoming."

John Wooden, American basketball coach and player

Take Action:

Are you currently being met with any hurdles or barriers? Think about where or who you can turn to for help or advice. Remember that there are no "wrong" decisions, everything happens for a reason. Take a deep breath and say out loud to yourself "**I've got this!**"

Journal Prompt:

Look back to a time when you were able to successfully pivot, change gears, or make new plans. How would you assess your reactions to the situation you were faced with? I'm willing to guess you made some impressive decisions, right?! Congratulate yourself on your ability to adapt.

STEP 4

FIND MEANINGFUL HAPPINESS IN WHAT YOU DO

Earlier, we talked about embracing the journey and overcoming the obstacles we might be facing. You might be thinking, "Sure. All that is nice. But I don't even know where I'm going!" Whether we're at a crossroads between two life decisions, we've reached a dead end, or we're standing in front of multiple pathways, it can surely feel daunting to have to decide where to go next.

Perhaps you've just quit your job and are considering shifting careers. Or you've moved to a new city with a chance to start from scratch. Maybe you've suffered loss or gained a new badge of honor.

Some of us were conditioned from a very young age to follow a certain path that our peers or family members might have set, only to find it wasn't something we wanted for ourselves. Others might have spent years hopping around, trying to find a point of stability.

I was perfectly content in my marketing career in the music industry. I took part in creating trailblazing technology for music, had exciting encounters, then jetted off to attend the biggest festivals and awards shows, even walking the red carpet.

And then, I became a mother. My two roles could not co-exist to my satisfaction. At that time, the music industry really wasn't set up to allow a mother who wanted to be there for her children the flexibility and solutions at work to make that happen.

My boss wasn't too happy about me being a new Mom, either. The burden of feeling I could not give my best in my career while being fully present for my child weighed heavily on me. Having had an absentee mother during my teenage years, due to her work, I knew the consequences it would have on my family if I followed the same path.

And so, one lunchtime, finally fed up with my boss' workplace bullying, I left the office—and never returned. It was such a spur of the moment decision, I even left my jacket on the back of my chair! I was on my way to becoming a fully-present mother, but I needed to do something more for me, too.

What about you? Do you know what's next for you?

Or, a better question: Do you know what gives you meaningful happiness?

Meaningful happiness arises when we find fulfillment in what we do. When we don't mind sacrificing our time and energy for something that gives us joy. When what we do creates an impact on the people who matter in our lives. **When we love what we do**.

Meaningful happiness comes from pursuing our passions, developing our skills and fulfilling our purpose.

"Purpose" does not have to be a grand feat. It can be anything, from innovating designs to mitigate climate change for future generations, to creating a home for your family. Your purpose is anything that is rewarding to you and your loved ones, and comes from deep within you.

So, even if you're unsure of where you want to go, you already know inside of you the person you are meant to be in this world.

The triumphs and trials I faced over the years helped shape who I would become and the new roles I would take. As I worked on my mental health and mended relationships (including with my incredible mother), I discovered that I was drawn to helping people who were struggling and had difficult backgrounds: from the marginalized and elderly, to those who have criminal records or have been abandoned in a time of need.

All these things have brought me to where I am today: hoping to empower as many people as I can reach, and help them find their authentic selves.

There are four things you can unravel in order to help you find your purpose: your core values, your passions, your unique traits, and your impact on the world.

Core values. A good way to start is by asking yourself: Who do I admire? Why? This can help you pinpoint what values you share with that person. Is it their integrity? Their work ethic? Their faith and loyalty?

Your belief systems are something ingrained within you through the years and, more often than not, unchanging. These are the foremost priorities that guide you in everything that you do. How much are you willing to sacrifice in order to live out these values? Would you quit your 9-to-5 in order to stand up to a dishonest boss? Would you give up your comfortable life in the city to care for your parents?

Passions. What gets you excited to start your day? What makes you feel alive? Is there something you can do for hours and not feel exhausted? What, or who will automatically put a smile on your face?

Unique traits. What are you good at? Is there something you can do easily? The people who know you best might be able to tell you what you're good at, or what they look up to you for. These characteristics and innate abilities are the tools that will help you in your future pursuits.

Figuring this out is particularly useful, too, if you're changing career paths. For example, you might have spent many years as an educator, but it's time to take on a new venture. Instead of looking at your accolades and the stacks of learning materials you've gained over the years, look into what made you a good educator: was it your ability to relate with the youth? Your patience and understanding? Your talent for taking complex information and simplifying it for others to understand? These traits might open new doors for you in a world outside academia.

Impact on the world. All pursuits are futile if they do not help your world in some way, shape, or form. Real fulfillment comes from not only rewarding yourself, but also from seeing other people be positively affected by your actions. In what ways would you like to help other people? Do you have advocacies or causes that you care deeply about? How do you want to be remembered? Again, none of this has to be grandiose! A simple "thank you" from someone you love may represent enough of an impact made by you.

As you grow your list, you'll be able to gather and synthesize the items that resonate with you the most. Putting your list together, this turns into your non-negotiables. Try creating a **purpose statement** that moves you and excites you.

This is the person you are already becoming. This is your **compass** that will navigate the road ahead.

With your purpose in mind, envision the life in front of you. How do you spend your time? What are the different roles you are playing? What's a typical day like for you? Who are the people around you? How does this image make you feel?

This image may be very near to, or very far from the life you are living right now. Along the way, you might get distracted, overwhelmed, or feel like giving up. It's important to have the big picture as your key focus. Your purpose statement can be something you tape onto your bathroom mirror so you can remind yourself every day.

Create a collage of pictures, words, or quotes that you can frame by your workspace. Prepare both your physical and mental space for what awaits you. Speak aloud as the person you are already becoming by using positive, empowering words. Of course, acting on your purpose is also a must. What do you need to change? What will you no longer tolerate? How can you hold yourself accountable?

By doing all these, you're turning your dreams into a reality and manifesting the life you want. Despite the hurdles, you will have these foundations as your anchor to strengthen you and your compass to guide you.

Finally, track your progress. One of the most powerful ways you can take control of your life is by keeping a log of your thoughts, feelings, triumphs, and yes, even failures. (We will cover this more in Step 7.) The changes might be small and the progress might be slow, but you'll soon realize, by flipping page after page of your log, you've come a long way from where you started.

Every step, after all, is a step forward.

Embrace the power that's naturally in you. Next, let's have a conversation on silencing your inner critic and accepting the person you are in this world.

Take Action:

Find a couple of people you trust and ask them what you're good at. Yes, it might be an awkward question at first, but you'll be surprised—they will likely have a perspective on you that you've never seen. Reflect on their answers as you begin to uncover your values, passions, traits, and impact on others.

Journal Prompt:

Being in a flow state is when you're performing an activity but time seems irrelevant because you're enjoying yourself, fully immersed in the task at hand and having a grand old time being in your zone! Start an ongoing list of five times you catch yourself *effortlessly* in a flow state over the coming days/weeks and what in particular you enjoyed about the task.

STEP 5

BE HAPPY IN YOUR OWN SKIN

From magazines and billboards to our own social media timelines, we're constantly being fed unrealistic expectations about what the "perfect you" should be like. Although I've noticed, over the years, that brands have begun to change their tone and embrace diversity (let us assume they are sincere in these efforts), it does feel a tad bit too late, doesn't it?

The fact is, so many of these expectations have become ingrained in ourselves, whether consciously or subconsciously, from when we were kids. Older generations might pass on traditions and stereotypical notions of what beauty means to them.

In children's books and primary classes, we might have been given false comparisons of what is beautiful versus what is ugly. Moving on to our teen years, reaching puberty, we find ourselves comparing how our bodies have changed with those of our peers.

High school was particularly tough for me. I was the only girl of color in my year and, unfortunately, that came with very few benefits (read: none)! There were no teachers of color and I was in a predominantly white area where I was often told I wasn't welcome. I couldn't even go home and see someone who looked like me in a book or magazine, or on TV. The same images were presented everywhere in my life: not me.

As young as 10 years old, I was aware that I looked "wrong". My skin was too dark, my hair much too curly and my body definitely did not look like a supermodel's. I couldn't get a boyfriend despite my "best" dance moves and overall popularity. There was pretty much nothing I could do to fit society's expectations of how I should look—and as a consequence my own expectations.

I did everything I could to change how I looked—often unconsciously. I used scalp-burning hair relaxers, hair extensions, and a myriad of lotions and tools to get my curly hair to appear straight. I went on every diet that came out (the Cabbage Soup Diet is just as awful as it sounds). I wore make-up even though I hated how it felt, battled with false lashes, whitened my teeth.

And yet, nothing I ever did made me feel like it was enough. It never made me feel like everyone else around me. It never made me feel like I was *perfect*. You, too, may have felt the same way, at one point or another. Many of us have insecurities about ourselves, from not having the "perfect" skin color, or the "right" weight, or the "normal" height.

But here's a lesson I learned along the way: I am actually just perfect exactly how I am.

I'm not like everyone else. I'm not "perfect".

But neither is anyone else!

If there is one thing you can take away from this, it's that **you're not like anybody else, and nobody else is like you.**

This can be challenging to accept and, admittedly, it takes time. Learning to love and accept yourself as you are also involves unlearning years of biases, trauma, and insecurity.

Once I began to see this as a lifelong process instead of an end goal, it became easier to absorb. This process of learning to accept myself includes creating constant reminders and practice, progressing deeper into self-love, and regularly nourishing my wellbeing. This isn't a sprint, and neither is it a marathon. In fact, it's taking small, careful steps, being mindful and aware of how I feel about myself, and ignoring any unnecessary noise that might take me back a few steps.

We can be our own worst critics. Negative self-talk, for one, is something we do far more often than we realize. These are thoughts that race through our minds throughout the day, sentences we blurt out during conversation, ideas that inhibit us from pursuing the things we want.

Try this: instead of using negative language such as "I can't" and "I'm not", use positive, empowering phrases like "I can" and "I am". How does it feel? In the beginning, you might feel like you're lying to yourself. You're not! You're just too used to the limiting beliefs that have been ingrained in you throughout the years. With practice, you will learn to let empowering statements be a part of you—and more importantly, you will start to believe they are true.

Look at yourself in the mirror and allow yourself to be your own person. Embrace yourself as you are, "flaws" and all, and let them be a part of you. Take a look, too, at what habits and behaviors you've been holding on to because you were unhappy with yourself. Get rid of the skinny jeans you've been keeping for a decade in the hopes you'll eventually fit back into them. Let go of your habit of binge-buying unnecessary beauty products every time you go to the drug store. Eat healthily, practice self-care, treat your body with respect, and take care of your wellbeing.

By the time I reached my mid-thirties, the abuse of my hair meant that a good portion of it, especially at the hairline, had considerably thinned out; it was traction alopecia, to be specific. I decided it was finally time to embrace my natural hair.

I worried that I would be looked at differently at work. I questioned whether my then boyfriend (he's still around) would accept the new natural look (he loves it). You know what happened? I ABSOLUTELY loved my true authentic hair. I saw it as the crown on my true authentic self. After I accepted my own hair (sounds crazy to say that, right?), I then started going without makeup—believe it or not, not one single person in my life has ever commented that my eyelashes are too short or that my lips need to be redder!

I started wearing the clothes I felt most comfortable in: I'm just not a heels girl, and that's okay! The best bit was ditching the decades of dieting. My body is my body. It will never look like another person's body. My nose is the perfect nose for me. My belly is just how it should look.

The truth is, out in the real world, nobody cares about your skin color or the shape of your nose. And if they do—are they the type of people worth having in your life?

Let me tell you how fulfilling and relieving it is to finally reach a point where I could look in the mirror and fully accept what I saw as exactly how it should be. It's still a steep hill to climb, but it's definitely freeing.

As you learn to accept and love yourself, you'll find your unique place in the world, head held high, with a smile on your face, ready to take on any challenge with "I can" and "I am". Even better is when this world accepts and loves you for who you are. We'll cover this more in the next step (hint: it's not on them to do so!).

Take Action:

Set aside 30 minutes, it's time for an online detox! On social media, the unfollow, hide, mute, and block buttons are there for a reason: to give you peace of mind. Get rid of the clutter that has been weighing you down and magnifying your insecurities. Unsubscribe from newsletters and shopping catalogs that make you want what you don't have. Then enjoy some screen-free time!

Journal Prompt:

Write a thank you letter to a part of your body you often have negative words or thoughts about. Appreciate the time that body part has stuck around, put in the work and helped to complete you. Express nothing but gratitude.

STEP 6

DON'T JUST FIT IN; BELONG IN YOUR WORLD

Have you ever been to a party or a club where you've felt so out of place? Maybe you're a little underdressed compared to everyone else. Maybe the vibe feels different, or you can't seem to find yourself in a pocket conversation that you can relate to.

We all move in and out of social circles throughout our lifetime, hoping to find relationships we can value and cherish. **Connecting with people** is simply part of human nature; it's something we crave.

We're built differently, though, in the ways that we connect. It might depend on our personality, upbringing, and the circumstances of a particular situation. Some people seem to blend into groups so easily. Some find their core group of friends and stick with them for many years. Others weave in and out of different circles, trying to find one that feels right for them.

Growing up regularly being in the minority, I had to work doubly hard to find circles where I could feel "accepted". Where I felt like I "fit in". But it wasn't until I became an adult that I learned that I shouldn't have to fit into my surroundings. Rather, the surroundings should **fit me**. The first is about "fitting in", the second is about "belonging".

Fitting in is changing yourself to be accepted by the people around you. It necessarily demands that you should be like everyone else. Therefore, it is inauthentic, uncomfortable, and betrays the person you are meant to be.

Belonging, on the other hand, is simply **being exactly who you are**. It necessarily demands that **you are unique and different**. It is about embracing yourself and letting yourself just be, and trusting that your environment will shapeshift and feel like home.

I'm extremely fortunate to have traveled extensively around the globe and also to have worked in many different types of organizations. In some places, I've felt unwelcome, especially as a female of color. In other places, I've felt as if I never want to leave.

My grandfather on my dad's side was a man called Jibril Martin. He was born in 1888 in a vibrant and exciting area of Lagos Island in Nigeria. His father, Jose Martin, was part of a group of liberated slaves who were taken to Brazil during slavery, but chose to return to Nigeria. They set up home close to the docks of Lagos where they arrived when they returned to the continent of Africa. These liberated slaves from Brazil held on to many traditions, surnames, and even architectural styles that they had grown accustomed to in Brazil.

In 2009, I found myself flying from Atlanta to Brazil to attend the Rio carnival. I'd always known I needed to go there. I didn't know why it was so important; I just thought it was a bucket list destination. Turns out, it was so much more than that. I felt at home. Immediately.

The people were out of this world, and they loved me instantly! They welcomed me and damn near worshiped me! While on the bus from the airport to our Copacabana beachfront hotel, I saw a street name. And right there it said MARTIN. My last name. I felt such an overwhelming sense of belonging that has never left me. The same belonging I feel when I visit family in Lagos.

When you belong in a place, a group of friends, a job, or a community, it will truly feel like this is where you are meant to be.

We've talked about accepting and being proud of your own skin. Part of embracing your true, authentic self is also recognizing, accepting, and being proud of your purpose and values. When you know who you are inside, it will be a lot easier to confidently tell the world: "This is me. I am who I am; take it, or leave it."

When you know who you are and why you are here, you become unstoppable.

Belonging can take many different shapes, but it's worth hunting this down in life, especially if you've been feeling out of place. Belong in your own body. Belong in your own home. Belong at work. You'll find a spot where you will feel safe, warm, and free from judgment.

We've spoken a bit on finding your purpose. Now, let's reframe the question: in what sort of world do you imagine your authentic self would shine? Maybe it's not the environment you're in today. Maybe it's time to take the bold step from doing karaoke nights to pursuing your dream of debuting on the live stage. Or, will you pick up a camera and shoot the film you've always envisioned in your head? Give yourself the tattoo you've always wanted? Explore new cities? Conquer your fears?

Your world will become an ocean that will envelop you. Take a dip; don't dive until you're comfortable. A baby's first steps, after all, are already an act of bravery. See how this world feels for you and how well it embraces you. Listen to your intuition: enjoy the moment and shut off the doubts that nag your brain. You are where you need to be.

This is your tribe, your home.

Go back to that memory of being at a party or club where you felt out of place. Look around you and recall the people who stood out. You'll likely remember the person dressed exactly how they wanted, dancing to their own beat, and not minding the people around them. It's pure and complete euphoria. They found a place to belong.

They could be you.

Exciting, isn't it? We've come so far from where we started. Next, let's put it all together and take the next step: the smallest, but most impactful task you can do.

Take Action:

Look up a local group or online community that you know you'll share common interests with. It can be a swimming club, an online forum for photographers, or a women's circle. Begin the research into where your tribe is currently gathering.

Journal Prompt:

Have you ever created a bucket list? Well, now's the time to create one, free from inhibitions, judgment, and limitations. Make a list of goals, dreams, actions that you would like to pursue. Do not think about what others would say. Ignore the inner voice holding you back. Find your freedom and identity within this list.

STEP 7

CREATE THE STORY OF YOUR LIFE

Doesn't it feel so much lighter, more invigorating, to accept that you are exactly where you need to be right now? To know that you can create your own path based on where you are meant to go? To imagine your world without inhibitions? To embrace a YOU that you love, and who is in charge every step of the way?

So far, we've covered six steps towards living true to your authentic self, in the way that you are meant to.

Begin by **enjoying the journey** and taking on a positive mindset for all that is to come. Understand that **stress is a natural occurrence** of your body, but there are many ways for you to mitigate it. Next, you can **overcome the obstacles** by accepting that life is never smooth-sailing. You can take a step back, assess, pivot, or restart. This is made much easier when you are able to **define your purpose** and find meaningful happiness in what you do. Your purpose is already embedded in you, so **accept yourself**, "imperfections" and all, and learn to love the person you are. You're the only person in this world who can be you; so **belong in this world** by being your authentic self.

So, what's next?

It's time to write your story.

Yes, literally *write*.

Imagine stepping out of your life for a bit.

You're an alien, looking into your world at this very moment. Who are you looking at? What are they surrounded by? What are your impressions of the scene you're looking at?

If you were to write a story from this point of view, what would you say? Would you admire the person you're observing? Would they make you smile? Would you shake your head and wonder why they behave the way they do?

Now, if you were to write the story of your past, how would you frame it?

And if you were to write the story of your future, who would you encounter?

The questions I've offered are little nuggets of thought for you to reflect on. Take a minute to pause and think about the stories you want to tell yourself, and how you want your narrative to play out.

After all, we're in the process of self-development. And development is the natural progression from one stage to the next. As you approach your new chapter, it would be a worthy investment to begin tracking your journey.

Do you recall your science class and lab experiments? I remember taking home bean seeds, some potting mix, and a paper cup. I had to keep a daily log of how much water I gave my plant, and what the weather was like. I watched impatiently, staring at the flatbed of earth, wondering how much longer it would take and what I might be doing wrong (or right!). Until finally—ah! Look, she's a seedling now. I continued to log details, including her height. In real time, I could not see progress. But through those activity sheets, I did.

People use journals in many different ways. Some have highly specific purposes to track a key area in their life, while others use it for more broad and encompassing reasons.

For example, if you're working on a career change, you can keep a log of your job search along with some important variables, such as key contacts you've met while networking. You can write free-flowing journal entries as part of your morning routine to reflect on the day ahead and set your intentions.

Or you can open up your journal as your wind down in the evening, to list how you are grateful for the day that just passed. You can keep a dream journal to help tap into your inner self. Or create a journal to plan your goals from the big picture down to the nitty gritty.

Whatever the purpose, journals are used to **find answers in the past, stay mindful of the present, and look forward to the future**.

Growth takes time, and impatience is likely. Journaling encourages you to pause and remind yourself where you are and how you are doing at this very moment.

It's a form of catharsis. When I journal, I include my thoughts, feelings, triumphs, and yes, even failures. In a sense, it's a way of problem solving. Without any judgment, I'm able to unload my brain and my heart of anything that might be burdening me. All these foggy thoughts and feelings are strung together into more coherent phrases. Then, I can observe how I choose my words, and learn to reframe the more negative and self-destructive narratives that tend to become second nature to most of us.

As you develop the habit of regular journaling, you start learning to tap into the subconscious and realize many things you might not know yet about yourself or the world. Journaling is a creative process, after all, and exercising this part of your brain unlocks so many potentials that might have always been blocked by the more logical side of you. You're free to dream, imagine, recall forgotten memories, and discover what invigorates your senses.

Over time, you might begin to see patterns of how you perceive yourself and the world. You might find a chain of causes and effects that could determine why you seem to be stuck. Do you have particular days where you feel extra irritable? Maybe you'll discover it's from the food you ate, or even from taking a particular route to work!

Regular journaling might feel daunting at first. The first question is always, "But what do I write?" Well, there are no strict rules to journaling. It has to feel comfortable, easy, and exciting. I personally love making it part of my daily ritual. After years of journaling, I've discovered that it has greatly improved my wellbeing and happiness. I've learned to process a bit of my past as well as mend relationships with others.

Even on my lowest days, journaling has always given me the safe space to grieve, rant, and fuss over all things big and small. But journaling has also trained me to pause, reflect, and reframe my thoughts to give myself some grace: always finding the positive, always giving myself hope. After all, if this is the story I tell myself, it must be a story I am proud of.

Are you ready to start telling yours?

Did you notice the action steps and prompts I left for you at the end of each step? Have you worked through them? If not, now is a good time to start! Pick up your favorite pen and a notebook of your choice and start logging your thoughts and feelings.

If you're keen to dive deeper into journaling, my book "How To Journal For Mental Health" is available for you to peruse. It's a comfortable read that is modern, research-backed, and encouraging. It's filled with numerous writing prompts to help you work towards being the best version of you!

"Keeping a journal will absolutely change your life in ways you've never imagined."

– Oprah Winfrey

Free Book Download

Improve the quality of your life and harness the power you have within you.

*****

Start your journey of self discovery and improvement with the modern, research-backed and life-changing book "How To Journal For Mental Health". Grab your FREE copy now: www.success-all.com/findingyourself

PLEASE LEAVE A REVIEW

Thank you so much for reading my book.

I've worked really hard to bring you a high quality, impactful and valuable short read. I also opened up about myself as I never have before. Yay to coming out of my comfort zone!

Behind the scenes I worked with an amazing team to copywrite, edit, design the cover and format the interior typography.

Time, passion and hard-earned personal funds have gone into creating the finished product. My inspiration and drive came from my goal to uplift and empower you, the reader.

It would mean the absolute world to me if you would leave a review on the online store where you bought this book or Goodreads if you got a copy elsewhere.

A positive online review will provide social proof and really help me reach more people.

If you have any criticisms, concerns or further thoughts to share with me directly, I welcome your email at hello@success-all.com

Your review will help me more than you can imagine and will definitely make my day. I thank you in advance.

Instagram

Facebook

Website

Printed in Great Britain
by Amazon

25806100R00046